TALES FROM *The Thousan*

Text adaptation and activities by Jennifer

Illustrated by **Alida Massari**

Editor: Victoria Bradshaw
Design and art direction: Nadia Maestri
Computer graphics: Simona Corniola
Picture research: Laura Lagomarsino

© 2006   Black Cat Publishing,
          an imprint of Cideb Editrice,
          Genoa, Canterbury

First edition : May 2006

Picture credits:
© North Wind Picture Archives / Alamy: 39 ; Private Collection / Bridgeman Art Library: 79.

We would be happy to receive your comments and suggestions, and give you any other information concerning our material.

editorial@blackcat-cideb.com
www.blackcat-cideb.com
www.cideb.it

CISQ CISQ CERT
TEXTBOOKS AND TEACHING MATERIALS
The quality of the publisher's design, production and sales processes has been certified to the standard of
UNI EN ISO 9001

ISBN 978-88-530-0518-2 Book
ISBN 978-88-530-0517-5 Book + audio CD/CD-ROM

Printed in Italy by Litoprint, Genoa

The CD contains an audio section (the recording of the text) and a CD-ROM section (additional fun games and activities that practice the four skills).
- To listen to the recording, insert the CD into your CD player and it will play as normal. You can also listen to the recording on your computer, by opening your usual CD player program.
- If you put the CD directly into the CD-ROM drive, the software will open automatically.

SYSTEM REQUIREMENTS for CD-ROM	
PC:	**Macintosh:**
- Intel Pentium II processor or above (Intel Pentium III recommended) - Windows 98,ME,2000 or XP - 64 Mb RAM (32 Mb RAM Memory free for the application) - SVGA monitor 800x600 screen 16 bit - Windows compatible 12X CD-ROM drive (24X recommended) - Audio card with speakers or headphones	- Power PC G3 processor or above (G4 recommended) - Mac OS 9.0 with CarbonLib or OSX - 64 Mb RAM (32 Mb RAM free for the application) - 800x600 screen resolution with thousands of colours - CD-ROM Drive 12X (24X recommended) - Speakers or headphones
All the trademarks above are copyright.	

Contents

KET   KET-style exercises

T: GRADE 4 Trinity-style exercises (Grade 4)

This text is recorded in full.

These symbols indicate the beginning and end of the passages
linked to the listening activities.

Introduction

The origins of *The Thousand and One Nights*

The Thousand and One Nights (in Arabic: *Alf Layla wa-Layla*), is a collection of stories from Persia, Arabia, India and Egypt. Nobody knows the exact age of these stories but a few of them are probably from the 9th century or before.

The name *The Thousand and One Nights* came from an Arabic translation of a Persian book of stories. The Persian book, now lost, was called *Hazar Afsana* (*A Thousand Legends*). It was translated from Persian into Arabic in about AD [1] 850 and the name *A Thousand Legends* changed to *A Thousand Nights* (in Arabic: *Alf Layla*). For Arabs, the number a thousand meant 'a lot', not literally 1,000. The Turks probably changed the number to 1,001 because this number meant 'a lot' for them.

The frame story 'Shahrayar and Shahrazad, his vizier's [2] daughter'

A frame story is the most important story in a collection. It continues through the book and brings all the other stories together.

The use of frame stories is very old. Collections of fairy stories from the Sanskrit period in India (about 200 BC – AD 1100) often had them: a well-known example is *Kathasarit Sagara* (*Ocean of Stories*), written in about AD 1070 by the Kashmiri poet Somadeva Bhatta. Other

---

1. **AD** : abbreviation for Anno Domini. A way of counting the years after Christ was born. BC : abbreviation for Before Christ. A way of counting the years before Christ was born. Note: non-Christians sometimes use CE (Common Era) instead of AD, and BCE (Before the Common Era) instead of BC. This system counts the years in the same way.
2. **vizier** : a man who advises the king in Muslim countries.

famous books with a frame story are *The Decameron* by the Italian writer Giovanni Boccaccio (1313-75) and *The Canterbury Tales* by the English writer Geoffrey Chaucer (about 1343-1400).

The frame story in *The Thousand and One Nights* is 'Shahrayar and Shahrazad, his vizier's daughter'. Shahrayar is a king who marries a new girl every night and then kills her in the morning. Shahrazad is his last wife. She tells him stories at night but always stops in the middle of one just before morning. The king doesn't kill her because he wants to hear the end of the story. This continues for many years. They have three children and in the end Shahrayar falls in love with

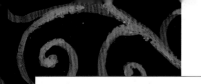

Shahrazad. The stories in *The Thousand and One Nights* are the ones Shahrazad tells Shahrayar.

The origin of 'Shahrayar and Shahrazad, his vizier's daughter' is probably Indian but the names of the characters are Persian. Shahrayar means *king* in Persian and Shahrazad, or Scheherazade (another spelling of her name), means *city-born*. Most of the other names in the stories are Arabic.

1 Answer the questions.

    1   What does the Arabic *Alf Layla wa-Layla* mean in English?

    2   When did the title *A Thousand Legends* become *A Thousand Nights*?

    3   *Kathasarit Sagara* is a collection of Indian fairy stories with a frame story. True or false?

    4   Who lived longer, Giovanni Boccaccio or Geoffrey Chaucer?

    5   Who tells the stories in *The Thousand and One Nights*?

    6   The frame story in *The Thousand and One Nights* is from Persia. True or false?

INTERNET PROJECT

Follow these instructions to be directed to the correct website. Connect to the Internet and go to www.blackcat-cideb.com. Insert the title or part of the title of the book into our search engine. Open the page for *Tales from The Thousand and One Nights*. Click on the project link @ . Go down the page until you find the title of this book and click on the links next to the @ .

▶ Read an Indian fairy story.
▶ Find out how many tales there are in *The Canterbury Tales*.
▶ Find out some information about Giovanni Boccaccio.

Tell the class what you have found out and read about.

THE STORY OF
SHAHRAYAR AND SHAHRAZAD,
HIS VIZIER'S DAUGHTER

Before you read

1 Match these sentences with the pictures.

1 ☐ The king, the vizier and all their servants left Samarkand and travelled for many days and nights.

2 ☐ Shahrayar and Shahzaman played chess.

3 ☐ Shahzaman told the vizier to put his tents in a big field outside the city walls.

4 ☐ Shahzaman opened the door and saw his wife in bed with one of the kitchen boys.

Now listen to Part One of the story and put the pictures (A-D) in order.

1 ....   2 ....   3 ....   4 ....

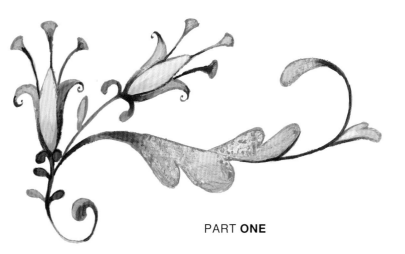

PART **ONE**

here were once two kings called Shahrayar and Shahzaman. They were brothers. Shahrayar was an important king. He ruled [1] all of Persia, India and China. Shahzaman, his younger brother, was the king of Samarkand.

One day Shahrayar said to his vizier, 'I'd like to see my brother. Go to his palace in Samarkand and invite him to India.'

The vizier (who had two daughters, Shahrazad and Dinarzad) made preparations for his long journey. He and his servants travelled day and night. When they arrived in Samarkand, the king greeted [2] the vizier warmly. 'Welcome to Samarkand!' he said. 'Tell me, how is my brother?'

'He is well, Your Majesty. But he'd like to see you again. He told me to invite you to India.'

'I'll prepare for the journey immediately,' said the king. 'You and your servants can put your tents in the big field outside the city walls. Wait for me there.'

---

1. **ruled** : controlled a country.
2. **greeted** : said 'Hello!', 'Good morning!' etc.

One evening ten days later Shahzaman arrived at the vizier's camp. 'We'll start our journey early tomorrow morning,' he told the vizier, and then he went to bed. At midnight the vizier received a visit from the king. 'I'd like to say goodbye to my wife one more time,' he said. 'I'm going to return to the city.'

Shahzaman rode back to the palace and went straight [1] to his wife's bedroom and opened the door. She was there in bed, but she wasn't alone. She was with one of the kitchen boys. Shahzaman was very angry. He took out his sword and killed both of them. Then he returned to the camp. The next day the king, the vizier and all their servants left Samarkand.

They travelled for many days and nights. Finally they arrived at the royal palace in India. Shahrayar came out to greet his brother. He was very happy to see him again. He gave him clean clothes, food and drink. He gave him a palace to stay in. 'That palace will be your home here,' he said. 'But you must come and see me every day.'

The two brothers spent the days pleasantly. They talked, played chess and walked in the gardens. But Shahzaman thought about his wife all the time. He was very sad. He stopped eating. He became thin and pale. [2] His brother was worried. 'Perhaps he wants to go home,' he thought. 'I'll send him back soon.'

One morning Shahrayar said, 'I'm going hunting [3] in the forest, brother. I'll be away for ten days. Would you like to come with me before you go back to Samarkand? '

'Thank you, brother, but I'm tired. You go. I'll stay here,' replied Shahzaman.

1. **straight** : immediately.
2. **pale** : without much colour.
3. **hunting** : chasing and killing wild animals as a sport.

He sat at his bedroom window all day. He thought about his wife and felt sad. He could see the garden of his brother's palace from his window. It was very beautiful There were trees and flowers. There were peacocks. There was a fountain. There were also two people in the garden that day, a man and a woman. They were kissing and laughing.

The Story of Shahrayar and Shahrazad, his Vizier's Daughter

Shahzaman looked at them carefully. The woman was his brother's wife and the man was one of her slaves! Shahzaman was very surprised. He thought, 'My brother's more important than me but he's unlucky with his wife too.' And he began to feel better. He started eating again.

Go back to the text

KET ❶ Are these sentences 'Right'(A) or 'Wrong' (B)? If there is not enough information to answer 'Right' (A) or 'Wrong (B), choose 'Doesn't say' (C). There is an example at the beginning (0).

0   Shahrayar was older than Shahzaman.
   Ⓐ Right   B Wrong   C Doesn't say

1   The vizier travelled to Samarkand alone.
   A Right   **B** Wrong   **C** Doesn't say

2   Shahzaman's wife was asleep in bed when he arrived to say goodbye.
   A Right   **B** Wrong   **C** Doesn't say

3   Shahzaman was tired and hungry after his long journey to India.
   A Right   **B** Wrong   **C** Doesn't say

4   Shahzaman stayed in a room in his brother's palace.
   A Right   **B** Wrong   **C** Doesn't say

5   Shahrayar was worried because his brother became thin and pale.
   A Right   **B** Wrong   **C** Doesn't say

6   Shahzaman was sad because he wanted to go home.
   A Right   **B** Wrong   **C** Doesn't say

7   Shahrayar went hunting in Samarkand.
   A Right   **B** Wrong   **C** Doesn't say

8   There were birds in Shahrayar's garden.
   A Right   **B** Wrong   **C** Doesn't say

❷ **Past forms of verbs**
Complete the table with the past forms of the verbs.

Infinitive	Past	Infinitive	Past
live		go	
travel		come	
kill		give	
show		think	
reply		sit	
start		feel	

3 Question words

Complete the questions with one of these question words. You must use one of the words TWICE.

What	Where	Why	Who	How

1 .... did Shahrayar live?
2 .... did his vizier go to Samarkand?
3 .... did Shahzaman kill?
4 .... did Shahrayar give his brother when he arrived?
5 .... did Shahzaman feel?
6 .... was kissing and laughing in the garden?

Match the questions to the answers below. Write the letter of the question in the box.

A ☐ Sad.   B ☐ His wife and a kitchen boy.
C ☐ In India.   D ☐ Shahrayar's wife and one of her slaves.
E ☐ To invite Shahrayar's brother to India.
F ☐ Clean clothes, food and drink.

T: GRADE 4

4 Portfolio — Invitations

You are going to see an Indian film at the cinema this weekend. Write an email to your friends to invite them to go with you. Tell them about the time of the film and the name of the cinema. Say what you are going to do after the film. (40-60 words)

Before you read

1 Listen to Part Two of the story. Are these sentences True (T), or (F) False?

	T	F
1 Shahrayar told his vizier to kill his wife and her slave.	☐	☐
2 Shahrayar's people were angry because he killed their daughters.	☐	☐
3 Shahrazad didn't want to marry the king.	☐	☐
4 Shahrayar asked Shahrazad to tell a story.	☐	☐
5 The king and Shahrazad had three children.	☐	☐

PART **TWO**

hen Shahrayar came back from hunting and saw his brother, he said, 'You are well now, brother. I am happy. Tell me, why were you so sad before?'

Shahzaman told him about his own wife and the kitchen boy. Then he told Shahrayar about his wife and her slave. Shahrayar loved his wife very much. He said, 'I don't believe you. My wife's a good woman.'

'Go hunting again tomorrow,' said his brother. 'But come back secretly in the evening. Then you'll see them.'

So the next day Shahrayar went to the forest. When it was dark, he returned on foot. In the morning the king went to his brother's room and looked down into the garden. His wife and her slave were there. They were kissing and laughing.

Shahrayar was very angry. He immediately called his vizier. 'Kill them both!' he said.

'Oh brother!' said Shahzaman. 'There are no good women in the world. They are all bad.'

THE STORY OF SHAHRAYAR AND SHAHRAZAD, HIS VIZIER'S DAUGHTER

'You are right, brother!' the king replied sadly.

Soon after this, Shahzaman went back to Samarkand.

One night a month or two later, Shahrayar said to his vizier, 'I want a new wife. Go and find one for me!' The vizier found a girl. He took her to the king's bedroom and Shahrayar married her. In the morning he said to his vizier, 'Now kill her!'

The next night he told his vizier to find him another girl. The vizier found one and Shahrayar married her. In the morning he told his vizier to kill her. Every night the king married a different girl and in the morning his vizier killed her. The people in the kingdom [1] became very angry with the king. They didn't like losing their daughters.

One day Shahrazad, the vizier's daughter, said, 'Father, I'd like to marry the king! I want to try to help our people.'

She was a very intelligent girl. She read and studied a lot and knew many things. But when her father heard this he was angry. 'You silly girl! The king will spend one night with you and then in the morning I'll have to kill you.'

'I want to help our people, father,' Shahrazad said. 'I have a plan. Please! Take me to the king.'

The vizier was sad but he took her to the king.

Later that night when the king and Shahrazad were in bed, she started crying. 'Why are you crying?' asked the king. 'I'd like to see my sister one more time before I die,' she said. So the king sent for her sister Dinarzad. When she arrived, she went and sat next to Shahrazad and said, 'Sister, tell me a story please. The night will pass more pleasantly.'

---

1. **kingdom** : country ruled by a king or queen.

Shahrazad began to tell a story. Dinarzad listened. The king wasn't tired so he listened too.

She told one story and started another one. But when she saw the first light of morning through the window, she stopped.

'I must know the end of that story,' said the king. 'You must finish it tomorrow.'

So her father didn't have to kill her in the morning.

THE STORY OF SHAHRAYAR AND SHAHRAZAD, HIS VIZIER'S DAUGHTER

The next night Shahrazad finished the story and started another one. She continued to tell the king stories for one thousand and one nights. During this time they had three children. Then one day the king said, 'You are a good and intelligent woman, Shahrazad. I will never kill you. You will be my queen.'

And they lived happily together for the rest of their lives.

Go back to the text

1 Put these sentences in order. Number them 1-10.

A ☐ After that, Shahrayar married a different girl every night and his vizier killed her in the morning.

B ☐ Shahrayar loved Shahrazad's stories and he learned to love her too.

C ☐ Every night Shahrazad told her husband a story.

D ☐ The vizier killed Shahrayar's wife and her slave.

E ☐ Some weeks later Shahrayar told his vizier to find him a new wife.

F ☐ Shahzaman told his brother about his wife and her slave.

G ☐ The vizier found a girl and the king married her that night.

H ☐ Shahrazad, the vizier's daughter, married the king.

I ☐ Shahrayar returned from hunting in the forest.

J ☐ The next morning, the king told his vizier to kill the girl.

2 Vocabulary

Match the words for men in column A
with the words for women in column B.

A		B	
1 ☐ king		A	niece
2 ☐ brother		B	aunt
3 ☐ son		C	girl
4 ☐ husband		D	queen
5 ☐ prince		E	daughter
6 ☐ uncle		F	sister
7 ☐ nephew		G	princess
8 ☐ boy		H	wife

3 Characters

Look at these sentences. Which characters in the story are they about?

| 1 Shahrayar | 2 Vizier | 3 Shahzaman |
| 4 Dinarzad | 5 Shahrazad | 6 Shahrayar's wife |

A He returned to his country.

B She met her lover in the garden.

C He wanted to marry again.

D He had two daughters.

E She knew many things.

F She liked listening to stories.

4 Adjectives

Find 14 adjectives from the story 'Shahrayar and Shahrazad, his vizier's daughter' in this word snake.

importantbigearlyangryhappysaddarkgoodintelligentsillytiredthinpaleunlucky

Say or tell?

Look at these examples of how we use these two verbs.

He **said that** he lived in India.　　He **told me that** he lived in India.

He **said**, 'Come and visit me one day.'　He **told me to** visit him one day.

'Don't worry about anything,' he **said**.　He **told me not to** worry about anything.

What did he **say to you**?　　　　What did he **tell you**?

We also use the verb *tell* before these words:

a story　　the time　　the truth　　a joke

5 Complete the rules with the verbs *say* and *tell*.

1 .... that...

2 .... somebody that...

3 .... something to somebody

4 .... somebody something

5 .... somebody to do something

6 .... somebody not to do something

7 .... 'Hello/Goodbye', etc.

6 Write the correct form of verb *say* or *tell* in the spaces.

1 Shahrayar .... his vizier to go to Samarkand.

2 'I'd like to .... goodbye to my wife one more time,' .... Shahzaman.

3 '................... me why you were sad, brother,' .... Shahrayar.

4 Shahzaman .... his brother the truth about his wife and her slave.

5 Shahrayar .... his vizier to kill his wife and his slave.

6 Shahzaman .... that all women were bad.

7 Shahrazad .... her father that she wanted to marry the king.

8 Dinarzad asked her sister to .... her a story.

THE
ENCHANTED HORSE

Before you read

1 Vocabulary

Look at these words.

> enchanted horse   fire-eater   snake-charmer
> small button   large terrace

Which of the people or things in the list above...

1   is part of a house or a garden? ....
2   is under a magic spell? ....
3   uses music to control an animal? ....
4   do you press to make a machine work? ....
5   performs a dangerous act, perhaps in a circus? ....

2 Listening

Listen to Part One of the story. ONE of the sentence endings is NOT correct. Mark the incorrect ending, A, B or C.

1   The Indian   A ☐ wanted to sell his horse.
                      B ☐ arrived during a celebration.
                      C ☐ was married.

2   The horse   A ☐ was made of wood.
                      B ☐ had black wings.
                      C ☐ wasn't a present for the king.

3   Prince Firouz   A ☐ told the horse to return to Schiraz.
                      B ☐ landed safely on the terrace of a palace.
                      C ☐ liked flying on the horse.

4   The princess   A ☐ was beautiful.
                      B ☐ wanted to help Prince Firouz.
                      C ☐ lived with her family.

PART **ONE**

t was New Year in the city of Schiraz in Persia. The city square was full of people. The king and his family were there too. There was music and dancing. There were fire-eaters and snake-charmers. And of course there was a lot of delicious food and drink.

Suddenly, an Indian man appeared in front of the king. He had a beautiful horse with him. It was made of black wood. The Indian spoke to the king.

'Your Majesty! This is a very special horse.'

'Really?' said the king. 'Why is it special? What can it do?'

'It can fly, Your Majesty. When I press this little button on its neck, it flies up into the air and takes me where I want to go.'

'Your horse is certainly a very special horse,' said the king. 'I'd like to have it for myself.'

'I'll sell it to you, Your Majesty.'

'And what's the price?' asked the king.

'Your daughter. I want to marry your daughter,' replied the Indian.

'That's a very high price for a horse.'

'It isn't a high price for a horse that can fly, Your Majesty. Try it and you'll see for yourself!'

'Let my son, Prince Firouz, try the horse,' said the king.

Prince Firouz immediately jumped on the horse's back and pressed the button on its neck. The horse flew up into the air, into the clouds and disappeared. The king was very angry. 'Where is my son?' he shouted. 'Bring him back!'

'I can't,' replied the Indian.

The king ordered his guards to put the Indian in prison. 'My guards will kill you if Prince Firouz isn't back in three months,' he said.

Meanwhile, the horse and the prince flew higher and higher. The prince was happy. He enjoyed flying on the horse. Then it began to get dark. 'It's late,' he thought. 'I must land.' [1] He looked carefully at the horse's neck and saw another little button. He pressed it and the horse landed on the terrace of a beautiful white palace.

He got off and looked around him. There was a small door in the corner of the terrace. He opened it and saw some stairs. He went down them and into a long hall with many doors. There was a light under one of them so he opened it. Six guards were asleep on the floor. The light was coming from a lamp in another room behind a curtain. Prince Firouz moved the curtain and looked in. He saw a big sofa and some women asleep around it. On the sofa there was a very beautiful girl. Prince Firouz touched her arm gently and she opened her eyes.

---

1. **land** : come down to the ground from the air.

'Don't be afraid!' he said. 'I'm the son of the king of Persia. I don't want to hurt you. I'm lost and in danger.'

'I'm the daughter of the Sultan [1] of Bengal,' said the princess. 'Don't worry! You're safe in my palace.'

Then she called one of her maids [2] and said to her, 'Give the prince some food and a bed. We'll talk in the morning.'

The princess thought about the handsome [3] young prince all night. The next morning she put on her most beautiful dress and finest jewels and went out into the garden. Prince Firouz was there.

He told her his story. 'Dear princess, I must return home to my father,' he said. 'He doesn't know that I'm here.' The princess was sad when she heard this. 'Can't you stay for just two more days?' she asked. 'I'm lonely here. My maids and the palace guards are my only companions.'

The prince looked at the sad face of the beautiful princess of Bengal and decided to stay.

1. **Sultan** : a person like a king in some Muslim countries.
2. **maids** : women who work in other people's houses.
3. **handsome** : attractive; good-looking.

Go back to the text

1 Answer these questions.

1 When did the Indian arrive in Schiraz?
2 Why was his horse special?
3 Did the king want to try the horse?
4 Did Prince Firouz tell the horse where to go?
5 Why did Prince Firouz want to land?
6 How many guards did Prince Firouz see in the palace?
7 What did the princess do when the prince touched her arm?
8 Why did Prince Firouz decide to stay in Bengal?

2 Negative sentences

Correct the information in these sentences about the story. Look at the example.

Example: It was Christmas. *It wasn't Christmas. It was New Year.*

1 The city square in Schiraz was empty.
....

2 An Indian man appeared in front of the queen.
....

3 The Indian man wanted to buy a horse.
....

4 The king was angry with Prince Firouz.
....

5 The horse landed in the garden of a beautiful white palace.
....

6 Prince Firouz touched the princess's face.
....

7 The princess thought about the horse all night.
....

8 Prince Firouz decided to go back to Persia.
....

29

3 Parts of a house

Match the parts of the house to the numbers in the picture. Use your dictionary to help.

- ☐ roof
- ☐ window
- ☐ wall
- ☐ bathroom

- ☐ chimney
- ☐ front door
- ☐ living room
- ☐ toilet

- ☐ garage
- ☐ stairs
- ☐ kitchen
- ☐ attic

- ☐ satellite dish
- ☐ hall
- ☐ bedroom
- ☐ cellar

PART **TWO**

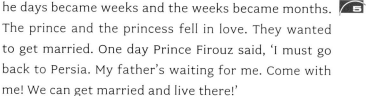

he days became weeks and the weeks became months. The prince and the princess fell in love. They wanted to get married. One day Prince Firouz said, 'I must go back to Persia. My father's waiting for me. Come with me! We can get married and live there!'

The princess agreed. So that night after dark they both got on the horse's back and flew across the skies to Persia. They landed in the garden of a small house outside the city. 'Stay here tonight,' he told her. 'I'll come for you tomorrow.' Then Prince Firouz went to his father's palace.

The king was very happy to see his son again. He told the guards to bring the Indian to him.

'Take your horse and never enter my kingdom again!' he said to him.

The Indian was angry with the king because he put him in prison. And he was angry with Prince Firouz because he took his horse. He wanted his revenge. [1]

The palace guards told the Indian that his horse was in a house outside the city, so he went there the next day. A servant

---

1. **revenge** : hurting (or punishing) someone because they hurt you in the past.

answered the door. The Indian said, 'The prince is waiting for the princess. She must come with me to the palace.'

A few moments later the princess was on the horse behind the Indian. They flew up into the air and in the direction of the palace. The prince and the king looked up and saw them. But the horse didn't land there. It flew over the palace and disappeared.

The prince was afraid. 'The princess is in danger. I must go and look for her immediately,' he said to his father.

The horse took the Indian and the princess to India. It landed in a forest near the Sultan of Cashmere's palace. The princess started shouting for help. The Sultan was hunting in the forest that day and he heard her. 'Perhaps that girl is in danger,' he thought. 'I must go and save her.'

When he saw the Indian, he pulled out his sword and killed him. Then he put the princess on his horse and they rode back to his palace.

Early the next morning the princess heard a lot of noise outside her room.

'What's that noise?' she asked a maid.

'The servants [1] are preparing for your wedding. Tomorrow you will marry the Sultan,' she said.

The princess was horrified. 'I must do something,' she thought. 'I can't marry the Sultan. I don't love him.'

She started shouting and crying and pulling her hair.

The maid was afraid. She went to the Sultan and said, 'The princess is ill. She can't marry you tomorrow.'

'Look after her,' he said. 'And we'll get married when she's better.'

---

1. **servants** : people who work in other people's houses.

But weeks and months passed. Many doctors came to see the princess but she didn't get better. Then one day a young doctor from Persia arrived at the palace gate. It was Prince Firouz. The princess was very happy to see him. 'We must escape,' the prince told her. 'And I have a plan. But first, you must stop crying and smile at the Sultan.' So the princess stopped crying and smiled at the Sultan. He was very happy. 'You are a very good doctor!' he said to Prince Firouz. 'The princess is well now. You can go home.'

'She isn't completely well,' the prince said. 'The enchanted horse put a magic spell on her. Bring the horse and the princess to the square this afternoon and I'll take away the spell. Tell all the people in the town to come and watch.'

At four o'clock that afternoon the city square was full of people. The Sultan and the princess were there too. When the guards brought the horse, Prince Firouz made four fires around it. He said some strange [1] words and threw some powder [2] into the fires. Suddenly, there was a lot of smoke. It was impossible to see anything. At that moment Prince Firouz and the princess jumped on the horse's back and the horse flew up into the air.

Soon they arrived at the king's palace in Schiraz. The king and his people were very happy to see them.

The next day the prince and the princess got married and they lived happily for the rest of their lives.

1. **strange** : not familiar; unusual.   2. **powder** :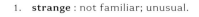

Go back to the text

1 **Word order in questions**

Put the words in the questions in the correct order. Then answer them.

1 return/the/How/and/Prince Firouz/Persia/princess/to/did?

2 angry/Indian/was/with/the/Why/Prince Firouz?

3 Indian/did/Why/Sultan/the/kill/the?

4 arrived/Who/at/day/the/palace/one/Sultan's?

5 Where/fires/make/Prince Firouz/the/four/did?

6 did/throw/Prince Firouz/on/fires/What/the?

2 **Joining ideas together**

Complete the sentences with *and, but* or *because*.

1 The prince and the princess were in love .... they wanted to get married.

2 The king told the Indian to go away .... he didn't give him his horse.

3 The Indian was angry .... the king put him in prison.

4 The Sultan of Cashmere killed the Indian .... took the princess to his palace.

5 The princess pretended to be ill .... she didn't want to marry the Sultan.

6 Many doctors came .... the princess didn't get better.

7 The prince threw some powder in the fires .... he wanted to make some smoke.

8 The prince and the princess flew back to Schiraz .... lived happily for the rest of their lives.

KET ③ Complete the conversation. What does the princess say to the doctor? Mark the correct letter A-H.

Doctor: Good morning, Your Highness. How are you today?

Princess: 1 ......F..............

Doctor: Oh dear! How long have you had it?

Princess: 2 ....

Doctor: I have some medicine for headaches in my bag. Here you are.

Princess: 3 ....

Doctor: Two big spoonfuls.

Princess: 4 ....

Doctor: Yes, but you should eat something first.

Princess: 5 ....

Doctor: Good. I'll go and ask the maid for a spoon.

Princess: 6 ....

A It's alright. There's one here.

B Fine. Can I have a bottle, please?

C I don't think so.

D I've just had breakfast.

E Since breakfast.

F Terrible! I've got a bad headache.

G Thank you. How much must I take?

H Can I take it now?

 INTERNET PROJECT

A flying horse in Greek mythology
Follow the instructions on page 6 to find the website you need, then answer these questions.
▶ What was the name of the flying horse in Greek mythology?
▶ Who wanted to ride it?
▶ What happened to him?
▶ What happened to the horse?

Versions of
The Thousand and One Nights

■he original version of *The Thousand and One Nights* is now lost but we know it was written at the end of the 13th century. It had 11 stories, including the frame story 'Shahrayar and Shahrazad, his Vizier's Daughter' and 'The Young King of the Black Islands'. People then began writing other versions of the stories in Syria and Egypt, and we have manuscripts [1] from both of these places.

The oldest manuscript we have is a Syrian manuscript. It is from the 14th century and is very similar to the lost 13th century version. It has the original 11 stories and is divided into about 282 nights. It is now in the Bibliothèque Nationale in Paris.

The Egyptian manuscripts we have are more recent: the oldest is from the 17th century. They have many more stories – Indian, Persian and Turkish – including 'The Voyages of Sindbad the Sailor' and 'The Enchanted Horse'.

European translations

A Frenchman, Antoine Galland, was the first person to translate the stories from Arabic into a European language in *Mille et Une Nuits* (1704-17). He translated from the 14th century Syrian manuscript but he made many changes to the text. He also added stories: 'Ali Baba and the Forty Thieves' and 'Aladdin', for example, are not included

---

1. **manuscripts** : old documents that were written by hand before printing was invented.

Open Sesame from **Ali Baba and the Forty Thieves**, illustration from **Stories from the Arabian Nights** (*c.* 1920) by Rose Yeatman Woolf.

in the original 11 stories. The first English translation came out between 1706 and 1708. It was very successful and soon there were many other translations. In 1800 there were more than eighty different collections of the stories. Perhaps the most famous, but not necessarily the best, translation in English is the one by Sir Richard Burton (1821-90), a British explorer and expert on the Orient.

Some film versions of *The Thousand and One Nights*

Date	Director	Name	Stars
1924	Raoul Walsh (1887-1980), American	*The Thief of Bagdad* silent film	Lotta Woods and Douglas Fairbanks
1940	Sir Alexander Korda (1893-1956), Hungarian-born British film director	*The Thief of Bagdad*	Miles Malleson and Lajos Biro
1974	Pier Paolo Pasolini (1922-75), Italian poet, novelist and film director	*Il Fiore delle Mille e Una Notte*	Ninetto Davoli and Franco Merli
1992	Disney Studios	*Aladdin* animated film	The voices of Scott Weinger and Robin Williams
2003	Dreamworks	*Sinbad: Legend of the Seven Seas* animated film	The voices of Brad Pitt and Catherine Zeta-Jones

1 Read these sentences and decide if they are true (T) or false (F).

		T	F

1   The original version of *The Thousand and One Nights* still exists.

2   There were 11 stories in the 13th century version.

3   The oldest existing manuscript is in a library in Paris.

4   The Egyptian manuscripts are similar to the 13th century version.

5   'Aladdin' is one of the stories in the 14th century Syrian manuscript.

6   The best English translation is probably not the most famous one.

7   Sir Alexander Korda was born in England

8   The film *Sinbad: Legend of the Seven Seas* is a cartoon.

Ali Baba and the Forty Thieves

Before you read

1 The words in exercises 1 and 2 are in Part One of the story of 'Ali Baba and the Forty Thieves'. Before you do exercise 1, look at the picture on pages 44 and 45. Then match one of these adjectives to each word. Write the adjectives in the spaces. You can find all the things in the picture.

<blockquote>

heavy   **silk**   **precious**   **gold**   **honest**   **black**

</blockquote>

1 .... jewels   2 .... coins   3 a .... saddlebag

4 an .... man   5 .... beards   6 .... cloth

2 Match the words with the pictures.

<blockquote>

cave   rock   ruby   sapphire   emerald
donkey   wax   scales   carpet

</blockquote>

42

PART **ONE**

asim and Ali Baba were brothers. They lived in a city in Persia. Kasim was rich. He had a shop. He bought and sold gold there. Ali Baba was poor. He collected wood in the forest and sold it in the city.

One day, while he was collecting wood, Ali Baba heard the sound of horses' hooves [1] in the distance. 'Who's coming here?' he asked himself. 'Perhaps they are thieves and want to steal [2] my wood. I'll hide in this tree.' He quickly climbed up the tree and hid in the branches. The horsemen arrived. Ali Baba counted forty men. They were big and strong and they had black beards. Each of them had a heavy saddlebag. 'I was right. They are thieves,' thought Ali Baba.

There was a big rock near the tree. The captain of the band of thieves went up to it and said, 'Open, sesame!' [3] Immediately, a

1. **hooves** : (singular hoof)
2. **steal** : take someone else's money, things, etc.
4. **Open, sesame!** : the magic words that opened the cave door. Sesame is a plant.

43

large door opened. They all went inside and the door in the rock closed behind them.

The captain and his men stayed in the cave for a long time. Ali Baba began to get tired. Suddenly the door opened and they came out. Their saddlebags were empty now. The captain said, 'Shut, sesame!' and the door closed and disappeared. Then they got on their horses and rode away.

Ali Baba climbed down the tree. 'I'll try those magic words. Perhaps there is treasure [1] in the cave,' he thought. 'Open, sesame!' he said, and the door in the rock opened. It wasn't very dark inside the cave so he could see well. There were bags of precious jewels — rubies, sapphires and emeralds. There were beautiful carpets and silk cloth. There were chests [2] full of gold and silver coins. Ali Baba went back to his donkeys, took his bags and went inside the cave.

He filled his bags as quickly as he could with coins. Then he hid them under some wood on his donkeys. 'Shut, sesame!' he said and the door closed.

When he arrived home and showed his wife the gold coins, her eyes became as big as dinner plates. She started counting them.

'Stupid woman!' said Ali Baba. 'Go and get the scales from your sister-in-law. We must weigh them. There are too many to count.'

Ali Baba's wife went to Kasim's house and asked for the scales. Her sister-in-law was surprised. 'Ali Baba is a poor man,' she thought. 'What does he want to weigh?' Before giving the scales to Ali Baba's wife, she took the cup and put some wax on the bottom of it.

 1. **treasure** :

 2. **chests** :

ALI BABA AND THE FORTY THIEVES

When Ali Baba's wife brought the scales back the next day, her sister-in-law looked at the cup carefully. There was a gold coin sticking to the wax. That evening she said to her husband, 'You think you are rich. But Ali Baba has more gold than you. He doesn't count his money. He weighs it!'

Kasim didn't sleep that night. He thought about his brother's gold. The next morning he went to Ali Baba's house and showed him the gold coin. He said, 'Brother, you say you are poor but I know that you weigh your gold. My wife found this coin in the cup of the scales. Where did you get it?'

Ali Baba was an honest man so he told Kasim about the cave in the forest.

When he heard about the treasure, Kasim wanted some of the gold too. Without saying anything to his wife or Ali Baba, he took ten donkeys, each with two bags, and went to the forest. He found the rock and said the magic words, 'Open, sesame!' The door opened. He went inside the cave and immediately started filling his bags with coins and jewels. While he was filling the last bag, he heard the sound of horses' hooves outside. 'The thieves!' he thought. 'What shall I do? They'll kill me. Where can I hide?' He looked around the cave but at that moment the door opened and the captain came in. Kasim tried to escape but the captain caught him and killed him with his sword.

'Perhaps other people know about the cave. We'll leave his body here as a warning [1] to them,' said the captain. He cut Kasim's body into four pieces and put them around the door of the cave. Then, after putting the gold and silver back in the chests, the captain and the thieves left.

---

1. **warning** : something that tells people about a possible danger.

Go back to the text

1 **Answer the questions about Part One of the story.**

1   What did Ali Baba do when he heard the sound of horses' hooves?
2   How did the captain enter the cave?
3   Why could Ali Baba see well in the cave?
4   Who had a set of scales?
5   How many bags did Kasim take to the forest?
6   Where did the captain put Kasim's body?

2 **Plurals**
Write the missing singular and plural forms of the words in the table.

singular	plural	singular	plural
	hooves	thief	
	rubies	body	
	donkeys	day	
	branches	cross	
	sapphires	piece	

Now write the missing forms of these words? They are all irregular!

singular	plural	singular	plural
	men		mice
	women		teeth
	children		feet
	people		

Past Simple and Past Continuous

One day, while he **_was collecting_** wood, Ali Baba **_heard_** the sound of horses' hooves in the distance.

Which of the underlined verbs is in the Past Simple tense?
Which tense is the other underlined verb in?
Which word combines the two actions?

- We use the Past Simple *(Ali Baba **heard** the sound)* to talk about an action that interrupted another action that was already in progress *(he **was collecting** wood)*.
- We use the word *while* to combine the two actions into one sentence.

While + was/were ...ing can be the first part of the sentence or the second part.

- If it is the first part, we must use a comma between the two parts. Compare:

*While he **was collecting** wood, Ali Baba **heard** the sound of horses' hooves.*

*Ali Baba **heard** the sound of horses' hooves while he **was collecting** wood.*

3 Put the verbs into the correct form — Past Simple or Past Continuous.

1 I .... *(meet)* my friend Max while I .... *(walk)* to school.

2 The teacher .... *(ask)* Yusuf a question while he ....
(write) a text message.

3 While Sami .... *(wait)* for the bus, it .... *(start)* to rain.

4 While Shahrazad .... *(tell)* a story, the king .... *(fall)*
asleep.

5 The captain .... *(arrive)* while Kasim .... *(fill)*
his bags with gold coins.

Before you read

1 What do you think happens in Part Two?
Answer Yes or No.

1 Ali Baba goes to the cave and finds Kasim's body.
2 The captain takes the treasure to another cave.
3 Ali Baba marries Kasim's wife.
4 The thieves have a party .
5 The captain kills two of his men.

Now read Part Two and check your ideas.

asim's wife was worried about her husband. He was late for dinner. She went to see Ali Baba. 'Brother-in-law,' she said, 'I'm worried about Kasim. He's very late. Please go and find him. Tell him that I'm waiting to serve dinner.'

Ali Baba knew that his brother liked gold. He thought, 'Perhaps Kasim is in the cave. I'll go there first.'

When he opened the door of the cave and saw the pieces of his brother's body around the door, he was afraid. 'The thieves will kill me next,' he thought. 'I must get out of here quickly.' Before he left, he filled his bags with gold and put them on his donkeys. Then he put Kasim's body in another bag and rode back to his sister-in-law's house.

One of Kasim's slaves opened the door. Her name was Morgiana. Ali Baba gave her the bag with Kasim's body and some instructions about the funeral. Then he went to see his sister-in-law. She cried when she heard that her husband was dead.

ALI BABA AND THE FORTY THIEVES

'Sister-in-law,' he said, 'we're in danger. Nobody must know how Kasim died. It must be a secret.' Then he told her about the treasure and the thieves. 'Don't worry!' he said, 'I'm rich now. I'll marry you and look after you. My wife and I will come and live in this house.' When Kasim's wife heard this, she stopped crying.

Morgiana was a clever girl. She understood Ali Baba's instructions about Kasim's funeral and she knew what to do. She went to see Baba Mustafa, the shoe-maker, in the market. She gave him a gold coin and said, 'I have a special job for you, Baba Mustafa. Cover your eyes with this cloth and come with me.' He was a poor man so he took the coin and covered his eyes. Morgiana took him through the streets of Baghdad to Kasim's house. When he took off the cloth, he was in a dark room.

'Sew [1] those pieces together again,' she said to him and pointed to the four pieces of Kasim's body on a table. 'Then make a bag for the body.'

Mustafa worked all day. When the body was in the bag, Morgiana gave Mustafa another gold coin, covered his eyes and took him back to his shop.

Three days after Kasim's funeral, Ali Baba moved into his house.

In the meantime, the thieves returned to the cave.

'Where is the body of that man? Where's our gold?' they asked angrily.

The captain said, 'Someone knows the magic words. We must find him and kill him before he steals the rest of our treasure.'

He told his best man to dress himself as a merchant and go to the city. 'Come back when you find the man who knows the magic words!' he said.

1.   sew :

It was early morning and still dark when the thief arrived in the market square. Only Mustafa was awake. He was sewing shoes outside his shop. 'How can you see to sew?' asked the thief. 'It's dark.'

'I am old but my eyes are still good,' replied Mustafa. 'Yesterday I sewed four pieces of a body together in a dark room.'

'Take me to that house and I'll give you these gold coins,' said the thief. Mustafa put the coins in his pocket. 'Follow me!' he said. He had a good memory so it wasn't difficult for him to remember the way.

When they arrived at Ali Baba's house, the thief took out a piece of white chalk and put a cross [1] on the door. Then he thanked Mustafa and rode back to the forest.

Morgiana returned home from the market. She was surprised to see the cross on the door. 'Perhaps someone wants to hurt my master,' she thought, and she put a white cross on all the other doors in the street. When the captain arrived and saw that there were white crosses on all the doors, he was angry. He rode back to the forest and killed his best man. The next day he sent his second best man to Mustafa. This time the thief put a red cross on the door. Morgiana saw the cross and put red crosses on all the other doors. When the captain arrived and saw that there were red crosses on all the doors, he was angrier than before. He rode back to the forest and killed his second best man. 'Tomorrow I will go and find this man's house,' he said.

When he returned from the city, he called his men together. 'We must kill this man and take back our gold and jewels,' he said. 'And I have a plan.'

1. **cross** :

Go back to the text

KET ❶ Choose the correct answer, A, B or C.

1 Ali Baba
   - A ☐ knew that Kasim was late for dinner.
   - B ☐ was worried about Kasim.
   - C ☐ thought that Kasim was in the cave.

2 Kasim's wife
   - A ☐ was in love with Ali Baba.
   - B ☐ was sad that her husband was dead.
   - C ☐ didn't want to marry Ali Baba.

3 Morgiana went to Baba Mustafa because
   - A ☐ she knew that he could sew well.
   - B ☐ he was her friend.
   - C ☐ she knew that he was poor.

4 Baba Mustafa took the captain's best
  man to Ali Baba's house because
   - A ☐ he needed the money.
   - B ☐ he wasn't an honest man.
   - C ☐ he had nothing to do that morning.

5 Morgiana
   - A ☐ didn't understand the meaning of the cross on
     the Ali Baba's door.
   - B ☐ was angry when she saw the cross.
   - C ☐ thought that Ali Baba was in danger.

❷ Take

Complete the sentences with one of these prepositions. In ONE of the
sentences, you don't need a preposition.

to   off   out of   back

1 'Taxi! Can you take me .... the Hilton Hotel, please?'
2 Karen took some cups .... the cupboard and put them on the
  table.

3 Jamil took .... his teacher some flowers.

4 Susie took her shoes .... because they were dirty.

5 'These new jeans are too small!' 'OK. I'll take them .... to the shop and change them.'

3 Fill in the spaces in the table.

	positive	negative			question
adjective	some	(not) any	*or*	no	any
people	1	(not) anybody	*or*	2	anybody
	someone	(not) 3	*or*	no-one	4 ....
things	something	(not) anything	*or*	5	6 ....
places	7	(not) anywhere	*or*	nowhere	8 ....

Complete the sentences with one of the words in the table.

1 It's a secret. .... must know about it.

2 There's .... sugar in these sweets. They're sugar-free.

3 I don't like cold weather. I want to live .... warmer.

4 Is there .... interesting on TV tonight?

4 Vocabulary

Use the clues to complete the puzzle and find the mystery word!

1 Mustafa covered his eyes with this

2 to put clothes on

3 the opposite of *stupid*

4 *in* .... means *not* safe

5 a shoemaker and a dressmaker can do this

6 Morgiana organised Kasim's ....

7 the past tense of *ride*

8 the captain's forty men

55

Before you read

1 These words are in Part Three of the story. Match the words with the pictures.

pan   tambourine   dagger   merchant   jar

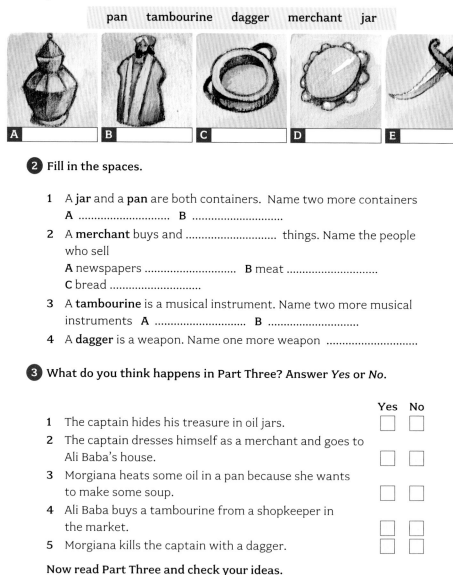

A .... B .... C .... D .... E ....

2 Fill in the spaces.

1 A **jar** and a **pan** are both containers. Name two more containers
    A ....   B ....

2 A **merchant** buys and .... things. Name the people
    who sell
    A newspapers ....   B meat ....
    C bread ....

3 A **tambourine** is a musical instrument. Name two more musical
    instruments A ....   B ....

4 A **dagger** is a weapon. Name one more weapon ....

3 What do you think happens in Part Three? Answer *Yes* or *No*.

<table>
<tr><td></td><td></td><td>Yes</td><td>No</td></tr>
<tr><td>1</td><td>The captain hides his treasure in oil jars.</td><td>☐</td><td>☐</td></tr>
<tr><td>2</td><td>The captain dresses himself as a merchant and goes to Ali Baba's house.</td><td>☐</td><td>☐</td></tr>
<tr><td>3</td><td>Morgiana heats some oil in a pan because she wants to make some soup.</td><td>☐</td><td>☐</td></tr>
<tr><td>4</td><td>Ali Baba buys a tambourine from a shopkeeper in the market.</td><td>☐</td><td>☐</td></tr>
<tr><td>5</td><td>Morgiana kills the captain with a dagger.</td><td>☐</td><td>☐</td></tr>
</table>

Now read Part Three and check your ideas.

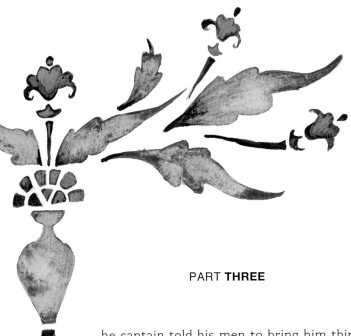

PART **THREE**

he captain told his men to bring him thirty-eight big oil jars. He filled one of the jars with oil and told his men to climb into the others. Then he put the jars on donkeys. He dressed himself as a merchant and rode to Ali Baba's house. Morgiana opened the door. 'I'm an oil merchant,' he said. 'All the hotels in the city are full and it's late. Can the master of the house give me a bed for the night?'

Ali Baba was happy to help the merchant. 'Tell him to leave his jars downstairs,' he said to Morgiana.

After dinner, the captain went downstairs and whispered to his men in the jars, 'When I say "It's time!", break the jars and come upstairs.' Then he went to bed.

Morgiana was in the kitchen. She wanted to make some soup but she didn't have any oil. 'The merchant's jars are full of oil,' she thought. 'I'll take some from one of them.' She took her pan and went downstairs.

While she was closing the door, a voice from inside one of the jars said, 'Is it time yet?' She was very surprised. She answered,

'No, it isn't time yet.' She went to another jar. A voice said, 'Is it time yet?' She gave the same answer as before. She went to the other jars, one by one.

She heard the same question from inside each one and she gave the same answer. Only one jar didn't speak. She opened it. It was full of oil. She filled her pan and went back upstairs. 'The merchant wants to kill my master,' she thought. 'I must do something.'

She heated the oil on the fire until it was very hot. Then she went downstairs and poured some of the boiling oil into each of the jars. 'Now we are all safe and I can sleep in peace,' Morgiana said to herself.

At midnight the captain came downstairs. 'It's time!' he whispered. Nothing happened. He opened one of the jars and looked inside. He was horrified! He looked inside the other jars. All his men were dead. Boiled in oil! 'Ali Baba is a dangerous man,' he thought, and he ran back to the forest.

Ali Baba saw the jars the next day and asked Morgiana, 'Why are the merchant's jars still here?'

Morgiana showed him the bodies in the jars. 'Well done! You are a very clever girl,' Ali Baba said.

Many months passed. The captain changed his name to Khawaja Husain and bought a shop in the market square. He sold the cloth and carpets from the cave. He became friends with the other shopkeepers. One of them was a young man.

One day Ali Baba visited the young man's shop. The captain saw him. Later he asked his young friend, 'Who was that man in your shop today?'

'That was my father, Ali Baba.' the boy replied.

The captain was surprised. 'That's interesting,' he thought. He still wanted to kill Ali Baba.

Some weeks after that, Ali Baba's son went to his father and said, 'Father, I would like to invite my friend, Khawaja Husain, to dinner tomorrow.'

'Of course,' replied Ali Baba. 'I'll ask Morgiana to make something special to eat.'

The next evening the captain arrived at Ali Baba's house.

When Morgiana saw him, she said to herself, 'This is the merchant who wanted to kill my master. He has another plot. [1] I must do something.'

She served dinner and then she put on a very beautiful dress. She went to the cook [2] and said, 'Tonight I'm going to dance for our master's guest and you're going to play the tambourine for me. Come! Let's go to them now.'

Morgiana danced some beautiful dances. The last one was very exciting. She had a dagger in her hand!

After this dance, Morgiana took the tambourine from the cook and went to the men. Both Ali Baba and his son put a gold coin in it. Then she went to the captain. He put his hand in his pocket to take out some money. But, just at that moment, Morgiana took her dagger and plunged it into his heart. He fell to the floor, dead!

Ali Baba was shocked. 'Morgiana! Why did you do that?' he said.

'He was the captain of the band of thieves and he wanted to kill you,' she replied.

She lifted the man's jacket and showed Ali Baba the knife in his belt.

'You are a very clever woman, Morgiana,' he said. Then he looked at his son and said to him, 'Son, you must marry Morgiana! She is the cleverest woman in Persia!'

---

1. **plot** : secret plan.   2. **cook** : the person who cooks.

Go back to the text

1 Look at these sentences from Part Three. Not all of them are correct. Tick (✓) the correct ones. Rewrite the incorrect ones.

A ☐ Ali Baba gave a merchant a bed for the night.
B ☐ The captain put a gold coin in the tambourine.
C ☐ The captain ran back to the forest because he was afraid of Ali Baba.
D ☐ When the captain came to dinner, Morgiana remembered his face.
E ☐ The captain filled thirty-eight of the jars with oil.
F ☐ Morgiana went downstairs because she wanted some water.
G ☐ Ali Baba went to the market place to see his son.
H ☐ After dinner Morgiana danced and the captain played the tambourine.

Now put the events in the order they happen in Part Three of the story.

1 ....   2 ....   3 ....   4 ....

5 ....   6 ....   7 ....   8 ....

2 Answer the questions.

1 Why did the captain go to Ali Baba's house dressed as a merchant?
2 How did Morgiana kill the thieves?
3 Who did the captain make friends with in the market square?
4 What was the captain doing when Morgiana killed him?
5 Why did Ali Baba tell his son to marry Morgiana?

3 Reporting orders
Look at this example.

*The captain **said** to his men, 'Climb into those oil jars!'*

*The captain **told** his men to climb into the oil jars.*

Rewrite these sentences using the verb *tell.*

1   Ali Baba said to Morgiana, 'Give the merchant some food!'
2   The captain said to his men, 'Break the jars and come upstairs!'
3   Ali Baba said to Morgiana, 'Prepare something special for dinner!'
4   Ali Baba said to his son, 'Marry Morgiana!'

4 Role-play
In a chemist shop. Work with a partner. One of you is the shop assistant, the other is the customer.

Shop Assistant : You have small and large tubes of toothpaste, shampoo for normal and dry hair and small packets of tissues. Decide how much each thing costs before you start. You start: 'Good morning! Can I help you?'

Customer : You want to buy some toothpaste, a bottle of shampoo and a box of tissues. Ask about the prices. Your partner will start.

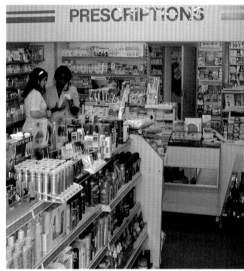

T: GRADE 4

5 Topic — Shops
Ask and answer these questions with another student.

• What time do shops open and close where you live?
• Are they open every day?
• What kind of shops are there near your house?
• Who does the shopping in your family?
• How often do you go to the shops?
• What is a department store? a shopping centre? a supermarket? a street market?

63

KET 5 Read the article about three famous women dancers. Choose the best word (A, B or C) for each space (1-8).

Isadora Duncan (1877-1927) was an American dancer. She didn't like traditional dances so she created her own free-style (**0**) .... dancing. She usually wore a long tunic, similar (**1**) .... the dresses of the ancient Greeks, and she didn't wear shoes. Her life was full of tragedy: her two children died in a car accident in 1913 and she (**2**) .... killed in another car accident in Nice, France.

Anna Pavlova (1881-1931) was Russian and the (**3**) .... famous classical ballerina of her time. She trained with the Imperial Ballet in St Petersburg, but in 1911 she

left (**4**) .... started her own ballet company. She travelled and danced all (**5**) .... the world.

The black American-born dancer and singer, **Josephine Baker** (1906-75), went to live in Paris in 1925 and became (**6**) .... French citizen in 1937. Afro-American culture was very popular in France in the 1920s and (**7**) .... she was an immediate success. In the 1930s she danced and sang at the Folies-Bergère theatre, and she (**8**) .... made some films.

0 (A) of	B with	C about
1 A as	B with	C to
2 A is	B was	C has
3 A very	B most	C more
4 A and	B but	C because
5 A through	B across	C over
6 A one	B a	C the
7 A that	B as	C so
8 A also	B usually	C has

THE SECOND VOYAGE OF
SINDBAD THE SAILOR

Before you read

1 Read these extracts from Part One of the story and match them to the pictures.

1 I packed my chest and travelled to the port of Basra.
2 I looked out to sea and saw my ship on the horizon.
3 When I got nearer, I saw it was a dome.
4 I quickly took off my turban and tied one end of it to the roc's foot and the other around my waist.

2 Look at the picture on page 69. Are these sentences True (T) or False (F)?

	T	F
1 Sindbad is sitting on a big rock.		
2 There aren't any trees or plants in the valley.		
3 The bird has a small snake in its talons.		

PART **ONE**

here was once a sailor from Baghdad called Sindbad. He made seven long voyages in his life. They were all full of adventures. He met many strange people and saw many strange things. When he was old, he liked telling people about his adventures and they liked listening. This is the story of his second voyage.

'When I returned home from my first voyage, I lived a comfortable life in the city for some years. Then I began to get bored. I dreamt of sailing the seas again. I wanted new adventures. One morning I packed my chest and travelled to the port of Basra.

'There was a good, strong ship in the harbour and it was ready to sail. I got on it. We travelled from port to port and from island to island. The other passengers on the ship were merchants and, when we stopped, they bought and sold things. Soon I began to do the same. Weeks and months passed pleasantly but without adventure.

'Then one day the wind took our ship to a strange and beautiful island. There were trees with delicious fruit, flowers of many colours, and streams [1] of sweet water. The air was full of the songs of birds, but there weren't any people. The other passengers started to explore the island. I was tired so I sat under a tree. I ate some of the delicious fruit from the trees and

1. **streams** : small rivers.

drank some of the sweet water from the streams. Then I fell asleep. When I woke up, I looked around. I was alone on the island! I looked out to sea and saw my ship on the horizon. [1] I began to feel afraid. "Oh, poor me!" I said. "What shall I do now?"

'I walked around the island for an hour or more. Then I climbed a tall tree. "I can get a better view of the island from the top of a tree," I thought. I looked left and right but I saw only trees, flowers, birds, the sea and the sky. Then I looked more carefully. There was a big, white object in the distance. I decided to go and have a look at it.

'When I got nearer, I saw that it was a dome. I touched it and walked round it. It was very smooth [2] and very big, but there were no doors or windows in it. Suddenly, it became dark. I looked up and I saw an enormous bird above me. It covered the sun. "A roc!" [3] I said to myself. "And this white dome is her egg." I remembered a travellers' story about these birds. It said that rocs caught elephants for their babies to eat. Just at that moment, the bird landed on top of her egg and soon she was asleep.

'I quickly took off my turban and tied one end of it to the roc's foot and the other around my waist.

'"Perhaps this bird will take me to a land where there are cities and people," I thought. I waited all night. In the morning the roc woke up and flew away and she took me with her.

'She didn't take me very far. We landed on the side of a mountain. I quickly untied my turban and hid behind a rock.

'The roc picked up a huge [4] snake in its talons and flew away. I looked around me. I saw a lot more snakes. They were sleeping among the rocks. "This is a terrible place," I thought. "There was fruit to eat and water to drink on the island. But there are only snakes here."'

1. **horizon** : where the sky meets the land.
2. **smooth** : completely flat.
3. **roc** : big mythological bird.
4. **huge** : very, very big.

Go back to the text

KET ❶ Choose the best answer, A, B or C to complete the sentences.

1 Sindbad went to Basra **A** ☐ to meet some merchants.
   B ☐ to look for a ship.
   C ☐ because he wanted to see the sea.

2 The island was probably **A** ☐ green.
   B ☐ dangerous.
   C ☐ quiet.

3 Sindbad climbed a tree **A** ☐ the flowers and trees.
   to look at **B** ☐ the rest of the island.
   C ☐ the white dome.

4 When Sindbad arrived **A** ☐ he saw that it was an egg.
   at the dome, **B** ☐ there was a bird sitting on it.
   C ☐ he looked for a door in it.

5 Rocs probably didn't eat **A** ☐ elephants.
   B ☐ travellers.
   C ☐ snakes.

❷ Descriptions

Can you remember the adjectives that were used in Part One of the story to describe the underlined words in these sentences?

1 Sindbad made seven .... voyages.
2 He met many .... people.
3 Sindbad lived a .... life in the city.
4 He wanted .... adventures.
5 He got on a good, ... ship.
6 The island was .... and ....
7 The fruit on the trees was ....

8   The <u>water</u> in the streams was ....

9   Sindbad climbed a .... <u>tree</u>.

10 The <u>dome</u> was ...., ... and very ....

11 The <u>bird</u> was ....

12 The roc picked up a .... <u>snake</u>.

 3 An island in the east

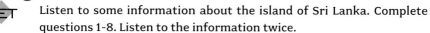 Listen to some information about the island of Sri Lanka. Complete questions 1-8. Listen to the information twice.

SRI LANKA

Position : **1**........................ of India

Size : greatest length **2**........................ kms

       greatest width **3**........................ kms

Largest city : **Colombo** on the west coast

Port towns : **Trincomalee** on the **4**................ coast

          Galle on the **5**................ coast

Geography : **in the south-central** : **6**................

          in the north : **7**................ and dry land

Highest mountain : **Pidurutalagala** : 2,524 m

Longest river : **Mahaweli Ganga** : **8**................ kms

  INTERNET PROJECT ◀◀◀

Find out more about the island of Sri Lanka. Follow the instructions on page 6 to find the website you need.

▶ You can see some photos of Sri Lanka.

▶ You can find a recipe for a Sri Lankan dish.

▶ You can hear the national anthem of Sri Lanka.

PART **TWO**

I walked down into the valley. There weren't any trees or flowers, only sand and rocks. The small stones under my feet sparkled in the sunshine. I looked at them more carefully. They weren't stones, they were diamonds! Then I knew where I was. "This is the Valley of Diamonds," I said to myself. "Nobody escapes from here!" I began to feel very afraid. I looked around. The snakes were still asleep among the rocks. Their bodies were as thick as tree trunks. [1] "They'll wake up when it is dark," I thought, "and come out to look for food. I must find a safe place to sleep tonight. Perhaps there are some caves here." It was beginning to get dark and I could hear the snakes. They were waking up. I walked faster. Soon I found a cave. It was big and dark inside but the floor was dry. "This is a good place to sleep," I thought. "I'll put a big rock in the mouth of the cave to keep the snakes out. I'll be safe here until the morning." I went in and looked around. At the back of the cave I could see two small red lights. Two eyes! There was a huge snake

1. **trunks** :

THE SECOND VOYAGE OF
SINDBAD THE SAILOR

there. She was sitting on her eggs. She was looking at me! I ran out of the cave. It was completely dark in the valley now and the snakes in the rocks were coming out. They made a terrible noise. I was very afraid. I decided to stay in the cave. "One snake is better than a hundred," I thought. "And she is more interested in her eggs than she is in me." So I found a rock and closed the cave. I was awake all night. I could hear the snakes outside. The noise was terrible. The snake at the back of the cave sat on her eggs and looked at me. When I saw the first light from the sun, I moved the rock and went out. It was quiet. The snakes were asleep so I left the cave and started walking down the valley.

'Suddenly, something fell out of the sky and landed at my feet. It was a big piece of meat. Then another piece of meat fell out of the sky. I was very surprised but I remembered another travellers' story about the Valley of Diamonds. The story said that diamond merchants never came into the valley because it was a very dangerous place, but they had a very clever way of getting the diamonds out. They stood on the tops of the mountains and threw big pieces of meat down into the valley. The meat was soft so the precious stones stuck to it. At midday rocs and eagles [1] flew down into the valley. They picked up the pieces of meat and carried them up to the tops of the mountains. When the birds landed, the merchants shouted loudly and made a lot of noise. The birds were afraid and flew away. Then the merchants took the diamonds out of the meat and put them into chests. This was the only way of getting the diamonds out of the valley. Later, the merchants sold the precious stones in the cities for a lot of money.

1. eagles :

'The story gave me an idea. I filled my pockets with the biggest diamonds I could find. Then I tied myself to a piece of meat with my turban. Soon an eagle came down. It picked up the piece of meat and me and flew up to the top of a mountain with it.

'As soon as we landed, there was a lot of noise and shouting. The bird was afraid and flew away. I untied myself quickly and started to run.

'"Hey you! Stop!" a man shouted. I stopped.

'"Don't hurt me, sir," I said. "I'm an honest man. I don't want your diamonds." I took three big diamonds out of my pocket. "Look!" I said, "Take these! I picked them up in the valley," and I gave him the stones. The man was very happy and thanked me. He took me to meet his friends. They were all diamond merchants. They gave me food and drink and listened to my story. One of them said, "You're the first man to escape from this valley."

'I travelled with them for many weeks. We visited many countries and we had many adventures. I gave them diamonds and they gave me food and drink.

'In one port there was a ship that was going to Basra. I was tired of travelling and I wanted to see my family again so I got on it. From Basra I travelled back to Baghdad. I was happy to be home again.

'I was a rich man. I gave many presents to my family and money to the poor people of the city. I enjoyed my comfortable life at home. But after a few years, I started to get bored. I wanted to travel the seas again and have new adventures!'

Go back to the text

KET ① Are these sentences 'Right'(A) or 'Wrong' (B)? If there is not enough information to answer 'Right' (A) or 'Wrong (B), choose 'Doesn't say' (C). There is an example at the beginning (0).

0 The roc left Sindbad in the valley.
A Right   **(B)** Wrong   **C** Doesn't say

1 This was Sindbad's first time in the Valley of Diamonds.
A Right   **B** Wrong   **C** Doesn't say

2 The snakes ate small animals at night.
A Right   **B** Wrong   **C** Doesn't say

3 The snake in the cave was asleep.
A Right   **B** Wrong   **C** Doesn't say

4 Sindbad knew a story about the Valley of Diamonds.
A Right   **B** Wrong   **C** Doesn't say

5 The diamond merchants threw the meat into the valley for the eagles.
A Right   **B** Wrong   **C** Doesn't say

6 Sindbad put three diamonds in his pocket.
A Right   **B** Wrong   **C** Doesn't say

7 Sindbad went to India with the merchants.
A Right   **B** Wrong   **C** Doesn't say

8 This was Sindbad's last adventure.
A Right   **B** Wrong   **C** Doesn't say

KET ② Complete this postcard from Sindbad in Sri Lanka to his brother Yusuf in Baghdad. Write ONE word for each space.

Wednesday

Dear Yusuf,

I arrived here (**0**) ...in...... Trincomalee two days (**1**) .... It's a very nice town and the people (**2**) .... very friendly. There are many interesting places (**3**) .... see. Yesterday I visited the Temple of the Tooth in (**4**) .... old city of Kandy. I am travelling with some merchants. I met (**5**) .... in the Valley of Diamonds. They are

(6) .... to stay here for the winter, but I want to return to Baghdad.
(7) .... is a ship to Basra that leaves on Saturday so I'm going to buy
my (8) .... tomorrow morning. I have a (9) .... of lovely presents
for you and Zubaida and the children. (10) .... you soon, your loving
brother, Sindbad.

3 Crossword

**Use the clues and the number of letters in the words in the (brackets)
to complete the crossword.**

Across	Down
he buys and sells things (8)	Sindbad wore one on his head (6)
precious stones (8)	there is one between two mountains (6)
a big bird (5)	an animal with a very long body (5)
ships stop here (4)	part of a tree (5)
a big box (5)	a big hole in a rock (4)

4 Opposites

**Write the opposites of these words. They are all in the story of 'The
Second Voyage of Sindbad the Sailor'.**

Verbs		Adjectives	
tie	1	dangerous	2 ....
take out of	3	asleep	4 ....
stay	5	interested	6 ....

Baghdad, the city of
The Thousand and
One Nights

Today Baghdad is the capital of Iraq. In the 8th century it was the capital city of the Abassid caliphs [1] and the jewel of the Near East. Caliphs who belonged to the Abassid family ruled the caliphate of Islam from 750 to 1258.

The second Abbasid caliph, al-Mansur (712-775), chose where to build the city. In 762 he started building his capital on the west bank [2] of the river Tigris. He called it Madinat-al-Salam (city of peace). It was also called the Round City because it was circular. The diameter of the city was 2,700 metres and it had three walls. The grand mosque [3] and caliph's palace, called the Golden Gate, were inside the first circle. The caliph's palace had a big green dome with a bronze [4] statue of a horseman on the top. The horseman moved when the wind changed direction. The caliph's army lived in the second circle and there were government offices in the third circle. The merchants' houses and bazaars [5] were outside the city walls.

Later, people started building on the east bank of the Tigris. This part of the city became bigger and bigger, and today it is the centre of modern Baghdad.

1. **caliphs** : Muslim rulers.
2. **bank** : high area of ground along the sides of a river.
3. **grand mosque** : an important religious building where Muslims go to pray.
4. **bronze** : a yellowish-brown metal.
5. **bazaar** : a place with many small shops and stalls usually in Middle Eastern countries or India.

Baghdad (19th century).

During the 500 years under the Abbasid caliphs, Baghdad was the most important cultural centre of Arab and Islamic civilization. It was also one of the greatest and richest cities in the world. It had museums, hospitals, libraries, and mosques. Teachers and students from many cultures and religions came to study at the Bayt al-Hikmah (House of Wisdom). They translated Greek manuscripts and studied the works of Aristotle, Plato, Hippocrates, Euclid, and Pythagoras. The most famous mathematician of the time, and the inventor of algebra, Al-Khawarizmi, studied there. The word 'algebra' comes from the name of his book *Kitab al-Jabr*.

Harun al-Rashid (766-809) was the fifth and most famous Abassid caliph. He ruled from 786 to 809. He appears in many of the stories in *The Thousand and One Nights*. It is possible that one or two of these stories were written while he was still alive.

Harun built many mosques and other beautiful buildings with the taxes [1] he received from the countries under his rule. He also built a beautiful palace for himself in Baghdad where he and his huge court [2] lived in great splendour. [3]

He loved poetry and music and he invited many poets and musicians from foreign countries to live and work at his court.

He was a good soldier and also a good ruler. He was interested in his people's happiness. He sometimes left his palace and walked around the streets of Baghdad at night. He liked talking to his people and listening to their problems.

There were long periods of peace in parts of the caliphate during the 23 years of Harun's reign but, after he died, there was a war between his two sons, and many buildings in the Round City were destroyed.

1 Complete the missing words in these sentences.

1 The Abbasids were a f............................ of caliphs who ruled for 500 years.

2 The Round City had a d............................ of 2,700 metres.

3 There was a s............................ of a horseman on the top of the caliph's palace.

4 Between 750 and 1258 Baghdad was an important c............................ centre.

5 Harun al-Rashid received t............................ from the countries under his rule.

6 There were many poets and musicians from f............................ countries at Harun's court.

7 Harun's r............................ lasted 23 years.

8 After Harun died, a lot of the Round City was destroyed in a w............................ .

1. **taxes** : money that people have to pay to a government or a ruler.
2. **court** : all the people who live in a royal palace.
3. **splendour** : magnificent and beautiful surroundings.

THE STORY OF THE YOUNG KING OF THE BLACK ISLANDS

Before you read

1 Here are four scenes from the story. Match them to the sentences (1-4).

1 ☐ Every night the queen put a sleeping potion in the king's wine.
2 ☐ The queen put a spell on the king and turned his legs into marble.
3 ☐ The young king married his cousin.
4 ☐ The queen went to the forest to meet her lover.

2 Work with a partner. In which order do you think the events happen?

PART **ONE**

hen King Mahmud of the Black Islands died, his young son became king. A few weeks later, he married his cousin. The young king loved his wife very much and he thought that she loved him. He was happy. But she was not a good wife and she didn't love him. She also had magic powers.

The king and the queen lived happily for five years. Then one afternoon the young king heard a conversation between two of his wife's maids. They didn't know that he was listening to them.

'It's sad that the queen doesn't love the king, isn't it?' one of them said.

'Yes, it is,' the other maid replied. 'She's a bad woman. Every night she puts a sleeping potion [1] in his wine. Then, when he is asleep, she goes out to meet her lover in the forest.'

The young king was horrified. He decided to watch his wife carefully.

That night he didn't drink his wine so he wasn't asleep when

---

1. **sleeping potion** : a magic drink that makes a person sleep.

the queen got out of bed and left the palace. He followed her to the forest. Her lover was there and they kissed passionately. When the young king saw them together, he was very angry. He took out his sword and hit the man on the neck. The man fell to the ground. Then the young king ran back to the palace before the queen had time to see his face.

The next morning the queen came to his room. She was wearing black clothes and she was crying.

'Husband,' she said. 'I'm mourning [1] my family. My father, my mother and my two brothers are all dead.'

The young king said nothing. He knew that it was not true.

The queen mourned for a year. At the end of this time, she built a black dome in the palace garden and filled it with precious carpets and paintings. Then she took her lover's body there. He wasn't dead, but he couldn't move or speak. She put him on a sofa in a dark room and built a beautiful fountain for him there. She went to see him every day and gave him soup and wine to drink. She cried all the time.

Three years passed. One day the young king went to the dome to speak to his wife. She was crying as usual. He was very angry.

'I'm tired of your tears!' he shouted and he took out his sword. 'You are a bad woman! I know that you keep your lover here.'

'Yes, I do,' the queen replied. 'I love him and I hate you!'

The king lifted his sword to kill her, but the queen put a magic spell on him before he could hit her. She turned his legs into a block of black marble. [2] He couldn't move.

Then she turned the four islands into four mountains, the city into a lake, and the people in the city into fish.

1. **mourning** : showing sadness when somebody dies.
2. **marble** : a very hard, cold rock.

Go back to the text

1 Answer the questions. Use short answers. If the answer is No, give the correct answer.

Examples: *Did the young king get married before his father died?*
No, he didn't. He got married after his father died.

Did the young king marry his cousin? Yes, he did.

1 Did the king and queen live happily for ten years?
2 Were the maids talking about the king?
3 Did the queen put a sleeping potion in the king's food?
4 Did the queen meet her lover in the palace?
5 Did the queen's lover hit the young king?
6 Was the queen wearing black clothes the next morning?
7 Did the queen build the black dome for her lover?
8 Was the queen's lover still alive?
9 Did the king go to the dome to see the queen's lover?
10 Did the queen put a spell on the king?

KET **2** Here is a conversation between two of the queen's maids. Choose the best reply. Mark A, B or C.

1 I'm tired today.
  A ☐ Are you?
  B ☐ What did you do?
  C ☐ Don't worry!

2 Shall we go and sit in the garden?
  A ☐ No, thank you.
  B ☐ Not at all.
  C ☐ It's too cold.

3 Would you like a cup of tea?
  A ☐ I haven't got one.
  B ☐ No, I don't.
  C ☐ Yes, please.

4 Your shoes are nice.
  A ☐ Thanks. They're new.
  B ☐ Yes, they are.
  C ☐ Here you are.

5 Have you made the queen's bed yet?

A ☐ Certainly.

B ☐ No, it's your turn.

C ☐ Yes, I did it.

3 Colourful names

Complete the names of these places with one of these colours. Then find them in an atlas or an encyclopaedia.

black   green   blue   red   orange   yellow

.... Sea   a long piece of water between Asia and Africa

.... land   a large island in the Arctic

.... stone National Park   the largest national park in the USA

.... Mountains   a mountain range in Australia

....   a town in France

.... Forest   a forest in south-west Germany

Before you read

1 Work with a partner. What do you think is going to happen in Part Two of the story? Choose A or B.

1 The young king is going to   A ☐ die.

                                 B ☐ meet somebody who helps him.

2 The queen isn't going to   A ☐ take the spell off her husband.

                                 B ☐ become a good person.

3 The queen's lover is going to   A ☐ die.

                                 B ☐ move and speak again.

4 The story is going to   A ☐ end happily.

                                 B ☐ end unhappily.

Now read Part Two and check your ideas.

PART **TWO**

fter that the queen visited the black dome every day. 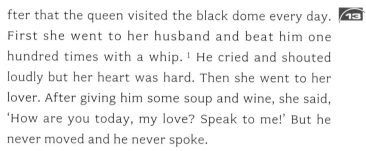 First she went to her husband and beat him one hundred times with a whip. [1] He cried and shouted loudly but her heart was hard. Then she went to her lover. After giving him some soup and wine, she said, 'How are you today, my love? Speak to me!' But he never moved and he never spoke.

Some years later, a king from a distant country travelled to the Black Islands. He went in the black dome and found the young king. When he heard his story, he felt very sorry for him. He promised to help him. 'I have a plan,' he said.

The next day, the king went to the room where the queen's lover was. He killed him with his sword and threw the body down a deep well. [2] Then he lay down on the sofa. Soon the queen arrived. She went to her husband and beat him one hundred times. After that she went to her lover's room. It was dark so she couldn't see the man on the sofa very well.

1. whip :   2. well :

THE STORY OF THE YOUNG KING OF THE BLACK ISLANDS

'How are you today, my love?' she said. 'Speak to me!'

The king answered, 'I'm very tired. When you beat your husband, he shouts very loudly and I can't sleep. Take the spell off. I don't want to hear him any more.'

The queen was very happy to hear her lover's voice again. She said, 'I'll take the spell off immediately, my love.' She went back to her husband's room and took a cup of water, which she heated on a fire. Then she said some magic words and threw the water over the block of marble.

'Now you are free,' she said. 'Go away from here and never come back.' The young king jumped for joy, [1] and the queen went back to her lover's room.

'My husband is free,' she said. 'Are you better now, my love?'

The king answered, 'I'm still tired. Every night at midnight the fish in the lake jump out of the water and cry and shout loudly. I can't sleep. Take the spell off. I don't want to hear them any more.'

The queen immediately ran to the lake and took the spell off. The fish became men, women and children again, and the lake became a city.

The queen went back to her lover's room and said, ' The people are free. Do you feel better now?'

'Come here,' said the king. 'Come closer.' The queen moved closer. Then the king suddenly jumped up and cut her body in half with his sword.

'The queen is dead,' he said to the young king. 'And your city and your people are free.'

The young king was very happy.

---

1. **jumped for joy** : jumped up and down with happiness.

'Why don't you come back with me to my country?' asked the king. 'I have no children of my own. You can be my son and rule my kingdom when I die.'

'Thank you, I will,' replied the young king immediately. 'I never want to leave you.'

THE STORY OF THE YOUNG KING OF THE BLACK ISLANDS

'Good!' said the king. 'I'll send my vizier to the Black Islands. He'll be a good Sultan.'

So the two kings made preparations for their long journey back to the king's country. They arrived safely and they both lived peacefully for the rest of their lives.

Go back to the text

1 Put the sentences in order and complete them with a verb from the list in the correct form.

> throw   make   go   find   kill   cut   take

A ☐ The king .... the queen's lover and .... his body down a well.

B ☐ The queen .... the spell off the young king.

C ☐ The two kings .... preparations for the long journey home.

D ☐ The queen .... to the dome every day to see her lover.

E ☐ A king from a distant country .... the young king in the dome.

F ☐ The king .... the queen's body in two pieces.

Multi-word verbs

*The queen **put** a magic spell **on** the young king.*

*She **turned** his legs **into** marble.*

*Later she **took** it **off**.*

These are 3 examples of multi-word verbs.

A multi-word verb is a verb (*put/take/look* etc.) + *in/out/off/up* etc.

More examples of multi-word verbs like **put** (sth) **on**, **turn** (sth/sb) **into** and **take** (sth) **off**:

* *If you don't understand a word, **look** it **up** in a dictionary.*
* *Before you buy those jeans, you should **try** them **on**.*
* *This meat is bad. I'm going to **throw** it **away**.*
* *If you make a mistake, **cross** it **out**.*
* ***Put** your books **away** now! It's time to go home.*
* *Jo **picked** the spider **up** and put it outside.*

2 Complete the sentences using one of the multi-word verbs in the grammar box. Use the pronouns *it* or *them*.

Example: Wow! I love your new coat? Can I *try it on?*

1   Your shoes are very dirty! .... before you come in!
2   If I take the shopping out of the bags, can you ...., please?
3   This chair is old and broken. Let's ....
4   Do you know Hari's telephone number or shall I .... in the telephone directory.
5   Tom, your clothes are all over the floor! ...., please!

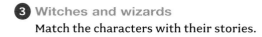

3 **Witches and wizards**
Match the characters with their stories.

Merlin	*The Lord of the Rings*
Circe	*Cinderella*
Gandalf	*The Arthurian Legend*
Professor McGonagall	*The Odyssey*
The Fairy Godmother	*Harry Potter and the Philosopher's Stone*

 INTERNET PROJECT

Follow the instructions on page 6 to find the website you need.
Find the answers to these questions about the witches and wizards in exercise 3.
▶ What did Circe turn men into?
▶ What magic trick does Merlin show Arthur how to do in the 1963 film *The Sword in the Stone?*
▶ When did Gandalf become Gandalf the White?
▶ What did Professor McGonagall teach at Hogwarts?
▶ What did the Fairy Godmother turn the pumpkin into?

1 Characters

Which people (A-J) are the sentences about?

1 Shahrayar and Shahrazad, his vizier's daughter
   A Shahrayar   **B** Shahrazad
2 The Enchanted Horse
   C Prince Firouz   **D** The princess of Bengal
3 Ali Baba and the Forty Thieves
   E Ali Baba   **F** Morgiana
4 The Second Voyage of Sindbad the Sailor
   G Sindbad   **H** Diamond merchants
5 The Young King of the Black Islands
   I The young king   **J** The young king's wife

Who...

1 climbed a tree?   ____ ____
2 danced with a dagger?   ____
3 didn't want to marry a Sultan?   ____
4 found a beautiful princess?   ____
5 gave money to poor people?   ____
6 had a bad wife?   ____
7 had magic powers?   ____
8 had more than one wife?   ____ ____
9 heard voices in jars?   ____
10 travelled a lot and had many adventures?   ____ ____
11 liked listening to stories?   ____
12 lived in a beautiful white palace?   ____
13 married his cousin?   ____
14 wanted to help the people in her country?   ____
15 put a sleeping potion in her husband's wine? ____
16 rode a flying horse?   ____ ____
17 threw big pieces of meat into a valley?   ____
18 told stories to save her life?   ____

2 Look at these sentences about the five stories. They are all incorrect. Rewrite them correctly.

1 Shahrayar's vizier had three daughters.
2 The Indian's horse was special because it was made of wood.
3 The captain's best man put a red cross on Ali Baba's door.
4 Morgiana killed the captain with a sword.
5 Sindbad climbed a mountain and saw a big white dome in the distance.
6 The Valley of Diamonds was full of flowers and trees.
7 The young king's wife built a black dome for her husband's body.

3 Prepositions
Complete the sentences with the correct proposition.

1 .... his bedroom window, Shahzaman could see the garden .... his brother's palace.
2 The captain put his hand in his pocket to take .... some money.
3 The queen filled the black dome .... precious carpets and paintings.
4 At midday rocs and eagles flew .... into the Valley of Diamonds and picked the meat ....
5 The Sultan put the princess .... his horse and they rode .... to his palace.
6 The captain and the thieves went into the cave and the door closed .... them.

The new structures introduced in this step of our READING & TRAINING series are listed below. Any one reader may not always include all of the structures listed, but it will certainly not include any structures from higher steps. Naturally, structures from lower steps will be included. For a complete list of all the structures used over all the six steps, consult the *Black Cat Guide to Graded Readers*, which is also available online at our website, www.blackcat-cideb.com or www.cideb.it.

Apart from the structural control, we also take great care to grade the vocabulary appropriately for each step.

Step One A2

All the structures used in the previous levels, plus the following:

Verb tenses
Present Simple
Present Continuous
Past Simple
Past Continuous
Future reference: Present Continuous; *going to*; *will*; Present Simple
Present Perfect Simple: indefinite past with *ever, never* (for experience)

Verb forms and patterns
Regular and common irregular verbs
Affirmative, negative, interrogative
Imperative: 2nd person; *let's*
Passive forms: Present Simple; Past Simple
Short answers
Infinitives after verbs and adjectives
Gerunds (verb + -*ing*) after prepositions and common verbs
Gerunds (verb + -*ing*) as subjects and objects

Modal verbs
Can: ability; requests; permission
Could: ability; requests
Will: future reference; offers; promises; predictions
Would … like: offers, requests
Shall: suggestions; offers
Should (present and future reference): advice
May (present and future reference): possibility
Must: personal obligation
Mustn't: prohibition
Have (got) to: external obligation
Need: necessity

Types of clause
Co-ordination: *but; and; or; and then*
Subordination (in the Present Simple or Present Continuous) after verbs such as: *to be sure; to know; to think; to believe; to hope; to say; to tell*
Subordination after: *because, when, if* (zero and 1st conditionals)
Defining relative clauses with: *who, which, that*, zero pronoun, *where*

Other
Zero, definite and indefinite articles
Possessive *'s* and *s'*
Countable and uncountable nouns
Some, any; much, many, a lot; (a) little, (a) few; all, every; etc.
Order of adjectives
Comparative and superlative of adjectives (regular and irregular)
Formation and comparative/superlative of adverbs (regular and irregular)

Available at Step One: